Investing For Beginners

A Beginner's Personal Financial Guide to Transform Your Life and Get Rich Before Retirement

Table of Contents

Introduction

Before getting started, I want to congratulate you on your decision to read this book. Some people will go their entire lives without putting effort towards a better future, but by just showing your curiosity regarding the world of investing, you are off to a great start with your money. My mission is to bring some financial awareness to people who seem to neglect and fear the topic of investments completely.

This is due to our education and culture, which is more saving and consuming oriented, and to the numerous political crises that we experienced during the past years, whether you're in Italy, the U.S., or where ever else you might be located. Saving for the future sometimes means acknowledging everything that has yet to come. When we do this, it can be scary and uncomfortable. Who knows where we'll be in 20 years, so why do we have to put money towards that time period when we can spend it on ourselves right now?

I believe that a single book can save a life, or at least change it. This happened to me when I discovered the power of investments and the culture of entrepreneurship, which is amazingly fun and truly self-oriented. The only thing holding you back from taking control over your finances is yourself. We're told sometimes that we're not good enough, rich enough, or smart enough to make our own money. We have to get rid of that mentality as soon as possible because we have so much power over our own money.

The beauty of being self-employed (even if this is just a second job, for now) is to experience what you would never feel otherwise, emotions, pain, fear, joy, anger and getting out of the comfort zone, which is my favorite way to grow and understand who I am. Investing itself can be an exciting business, but when we get to take control over ourselves, this is when we start to experience true freedom.

It all starts with you taking care of your finances. Many people just want to ensure that they make enough money to get by. Some people are satisfied with not making more and just having enough to get by. This is a fine way to live, but when we take control of our own money, we can improve the quality of life we have by eliminating stress and worry over where our next meal is going to come from. If you don't need a lot in your life to feel satisfied, that's great, but what about when we run into emergencies? Sometimes, there might be a time we have to go to the hospital or replace something that isn't covered by insurance. Our pets can get sick as well, and we won't always have the money to take care of them. In some cases, we might lose our jobs without any warning, so it is always best that we have more money than just what we need.

Investing in yourself is a great way to start. Maybe it is a talent you have, a skill you've acquired, or just an area that you are very knowledgeable in. No matter what that might entail, you have the power to make money on your own, so why not invest in that power as well. It is easy to get in business with other people at the start, but down the road, there are a ton of different issues you risk running into. If you instead take charge over your own finances, you can better ensure that you are maintaining a healthy amount of control over your business and not have to worry about anyone else affecting that.

The right mindset will also help make sure that you are going to have control over how you are making money. You might have a lot of money and know plenty of people to get you started with investing, but if your mindset is all wrong, you are not going to be making as much money as you could hope for.

Another important step is to start sooner rather than later. You also want to make sure that you are starting off small. The sooner you start, the more you'll have in the end. It can be a hard thing to get started with as well, as it is a habit that will take time. Instead of waiting until you are 10 years away from retirement to start saving, you should aim to do it ASAP so that you don't have to worry whether or not you'll have enough.

Always keep in mind diversification, a term we'll be discussing in the last chapter. The more variety you can bring into your investments, the less chance of loss there will be. If you make sure you are keeping an open mind and trying new things, you'll run into more opportunities that can help take your money from an average income to something much greater.

Therefore, my goal for this project is to create a sense of interest in investments and show how these can add value to your life. Don't be afraid of your own money and your future. Embrace it and let it become an important part of your life. Imagine if we had started investing since we got money from our grandparents or the tooth fairy.

If you invested $100 in your saving since you were 5, and you are now 30, that's an extra $2500 right now, plus however much interest it might have made. That's a lot of money, but as adults, we have the power to give much more than $100 a year, along with a sense of finding investments with greater returns than just our savings account. I'm going to take you through the beginning stages of investment in the next five chapters, including taking control, investing in yourself, starting saving now, and diversifying your investments.

Chapter 1 – Taking Control of Your Finances

"There is no better learning than that which comes from experiences and quality reflections on those experiences." – Ray Dalio

We don't always realize how much we might be sabotaging our own finances. Sometimes, it might feel as though we're doing the right thing, but we end up making a decision that disrupts the track towards making real money that's actually worth something. If we focus too much on what other people are doing and don't look out for our own financial stability, we can end up losing money faster than we make it. Money isn't everything, and we shouldn't all have to think about it constantly. What we do deserve is a secure way to make money without having to constantly stress over where our next paycheck is coming from. When we learn how to start investing our money wisely, we can end up making more and more of it without having to put as much effort into the actual "labor" part.

The first step is creating a budget. This is how much you can spend in a week, month, and year. Whether you make a salary or your income changes from week to week, it starts by determining your weekly average of money coming in, with taxes in consideration. Most of us get taxes taken out of our wages, but some people have to file their income separately and pay taxes later on. After taxes have been figured out, it is time that we look at how much money has to go towards utilities. It is important that we're making twice as much a month that it takes to pay off all of our monthly requirements, which includes rent or mortgage, electric, internet/cable, water, waste, gas, credit card payments, and any other charges or fees that we have to look out for monthly. What's leftover is money that goes towards the basic functions of living, such as groceries, toiletries, and other day to day supplies. We have to make sure that we cut both of those aspects down, both utility and function, in order to have a certain amount left that goes towards savings.

Setting realistic goals is important when it comes to budgeting. You can't say that you are going to save half of your monthly income if you don't even make twice as much as what it costs to stay alive. Sometimes, we set really unrealistic goals that sound great, but they're unmanageable and almost impossible to actually reach. This is because we want to fantasize about the end result rather than take responsibility for actually meeting and making these goals. When we set these unrealistic goals, we end up setting ourselves up for failure, which leads to disappointment, which leads to discouragement and an overall lack of motivation. It can be challenging to pick back up and try again if we feel as though we're continually failing. In order to make sure that we don't put ourselves in a situation that kills our self-esteem, we have to recognize that it all starts with being realistic and practical with the goals that we decide to set for ourselves.

Look at how much money is spent on your food. It can start as simply as cutting down your grocery budget. Do you eat out more often than you cook at home? Do you buy expensive fast food instead of creating meals that last you throughout the week? Start first by making sure that you are eating meals made from food purchased at a grocery store more often than you're eating food you bought at a restaurant. The appeal of eating out is high because you get to eat a meal that was crafted by someone else.

Build Your Way to Investing

Investing is a way to expand on your income. When you have enough money to put away in your savings, pay your regular bills, and still have some leftover, then you can put that extra money towards a project that could potentially double that amount. Investing can be done either largely or in a smaller way, and no matter what you choose, it is possible to make extra money just with the cash that you have leftover.

You can start with this as a side job, but it might eventually grow to be your main source of income. Maybe you invest in something that has a return of around $500 a month. If that doubles every year, soon you'll be making $16,000 in five years of that investment. This isn't always the case for all businesses, but it can be a great way to use the money you already have to turn it into even more cash.

It is income that helps to plan for the future. When you have an investment, it is not like you are going to buy something and see the return that day. An investment is more of a way to get yourself set up for the future. You'll be able to better take charge of your finances because you can look at 6 months, 12 months, and 24 months into the future and know where some of your income is going to be coming from. The end goal is to eventually have enough investments that you don't have to worry about any other forms of employment.

There are many forms of investing. You might invest in yourself, or a skill/talent that you have. Maybe you know someone personally that's looking for investors, or you come in contact with another business online. You could invest in stocks or real estate, two lucrative businesses that will be around for a while.

Investing will help you with retirement as well as your taxes.

When you make an investment, depending on the kind, you can sometimes get tax breaks, or you at least don't have to worry about paying certain taxes until you've started spending the money that's made from the investments. You can put your money towards a traditional IRA, SEP IRA, or a 401k, and you'll end up not having to get taxed on the year in which you earned it. Instead, you do when you retire.

The money is doing the work for you. You don't have to clock into a job every day and work for minimum wages from someone that does hardly any work at all. You get to be in charge of your own money, and you have the ability to take control back over yourself. For too long we've worked for people that only have to pay us as little as possible while they make all the money. Now it is our turn to make all the money on our own without having to live by someone else's rules.

It becomes a passive income. If you've invested in real estate, you can make money without even having to do anything. If you do have to put some labor towards a position, you can hire someone to do the things you don't want to do, such as invoicing, organizing files, taxation, and other forms of management that might require you to work consistent hours. Instead of spending all your time at a place you dislike, you get to make your own money now without even having to clock in.

It is a security blanket. You can use your investments as reminders that you are going to be getting more money in. Sometimes, investments can be risky, but if we make sure we're only putting our money towards something smart, we don't have to worry about the risks as much. Some people enjoy the risks that come along with higher investments, and many people have the patience to play it safe and earn their money over a longer period of time.

Cutting the Unnecessary

In order to take control of your finances, you have to look at what you might have been spending money on that is unnecessary. There are plenty of costs in our life that we don't always realize are completely unnecessary. Some people don't even stop to think about what they're spending their money on and how much they could save if they just chose to cut that cost out completely. Other people will mindlessly keep spending wondering where their money is going without actually looking at the things they keep buying that are completely unnecessary.

Look at the way in which you use transportation. Do you have a car to take you to work, school, and everywhere else you need to go? Some people live in areas where cars are completely necessary, but other people choose cars over their public transportation every single day, even though it costs them so much more money. Instead of continually using your car, try cutting down usage so that you can save some money on gas, tolls, and parking. If you drive to work every day and have to pay a parking fee, already you are saving a ton of money over the week. If you need your car to get anywhere, ask yourself if the car you have is the right one. Some people feel the need to buy higher-end cars, bigger vehicles, and gas guzzlers that make their weekly transportation costs so much higher.

Cable and internet can be expensive costs that we don't always utilize. Is it really necessary to pay over $100 a month just so you can get one channel that you watch consistently? Services like Netflix, Hulu, HBO go, and other streaming services offer plenty of options rather than the cable that's filled with commercials and spotty with how much is actually provided. If you have cable just to watch something specific, look at how much it would cost to purchase a DVD or Blu-ray of that viewing, or if you can just pay for a one time viewing rather than having to pay for the channel consistently. These two things can really help lighten your load if you cut down on their weekly costs.

Bad habits can lead to unnecessary costs. Think about how you shop. Do you plan things out when you go to the store, or are you more reliant just on seeing what you like, or looking at what's on sale? If you don't have a plan when you go to the store, you end up spending way more than you intended to, and you'll buy unnecessary things that just end up going to waste.

There is always room to save a little money. Even if you are barely scraping by, there's something you can cut out that will help you to save money in the long run. Maybe it is a morning coffee, or even just buying ice cream every time you grocery shop. Saving just $5 a week means that you'll have $260 at the end of the year. It might not be that much to some, but then imagine doubling that $260 every year with an investment. After 10 years, your investment could be over $100,000 if you made an investment that increases by %200 every year.

Sometimes saving money means that you have to group different expenses together. Though you might be paying a little more than your minimum payment, and you are up to date with all your bills, this does not mean that you are being as smart as possible with your finances. There still might be an area where you can make an improvement.

Consolidate

When people think of consolidation, they usually think about someone that takes a loan out to pay all their credit cards at once so you can then only make one monthly payment on that loan. This is a form of consolidation, but it is not the only one. Doing this can still be pretty helpful, as instead of making 5 different $50 payments on credit cards that all have different interest rates, you can pay $200 a month on a loan that has a lower interest payment than all the credit cards combined. If this is possible for you, it is certainly something that you should consider. If not, there are other ways that you can consolidate.

You might be able to consolidate with your retirement fund. Just make sure you are financially stable before you decide to do this. Sometimes, our retirement fund is just sitting there, and it might not be getting as much interest as we are paying for our credit cards. So, if your credit cards are gaining 20% interest every year, and you have $10,000 in credit card debt, you are going to get a lot of debt built up if you are just making the minimum payments. Then, maybe you have a retirement fund that currently holds $35,000. It might be something of interest for you to pay off those credit cards and instead of making payments on the credit cards, you make payments back to the retirement fund so that there's no more interest being added onto the debt you already have to pay.

Look for other ways of consolidation. This might be in the other bills you pay as well. Can you bundle any services that you are paying for? Can you cut some out for an alternative that gives you more? Maybe this is with your cell phone bills or your internet services. Look for other people you can share responsibilities with, even if they don't live with you. As long as someone is trustworthy, they could end up helping you to save money if you both combine payments to cut down your overall costs together.

Think of beauty habits. Do you have to buy expensive new makeup every week, or even get your nails done too often? Perhaps your haircuts are expensive, and even look at the way that you get your dogs groomed. We feel a lot of pressure to keep up with our beauty habits and giving up on some expensive treatments does not always mean that we'll be giving up on ourselves. Sometimes, you just have to look at things involved with vanity to save a few extra dollars.

There are other forms of spending in our lives that we can try and consolidate. Instead of spending money on going out to eat and going grocery shopping a few times a week, look at stores like Costco or Sam's Club where you can buy things in bulk, so you only have to go twice a month. The less you force yourself to go to the store to buy certain things, the easier it will be to resist temptation and stick to a cost-efficient meal plan.

All of these techniques go to helping you make more money as an investor. When you save money, you have more that can go towards investing. Instead of spending $20 on a meal that you are going to eat and forget about, you can put that $20 towards a $200 investment that ends up doubling throughout the years and making you a ton of extra cash. Though it can be hard to say no to life's luxuries, it is the best way to save money in the end.

Saving Ten Percent of Your Income

Saving is important for your future. Spending right now is fun but saving for later is the smart decision. It seems as though we live in a society where saving is less and less important, and people would rather put themselves in massive and dangerous debt than even think about starting a retirement fund. Retirement is important because we shouldn't have to work up until the day that we die. Some people think that they'll be able to do so, or that they'll want to keep working. It is true that retirement isn't for everyone, but sometimes, we have to go into retirement because of our health. As we get older, we're more susceptible to breaking major parts of our bodies, like our hips, backs, and legs. It is unfortunate, but an injury like this can put us out of work when we reach 70 or older. We are also at a higher risk of illnesses like heart and lung disease, or mind-altering sicknesses like Alzheimer's and dementia. Though we can do a lot to try and prevent these things, they can be unavoidable. Though you might not want to have to retire, you have to be realistic and save for an emergency or health condition that takes away your ability to work.

There's a good chance you are not even using 90 percent on the most basic things to get by. If you consolidate and cut costs, you'll likely have more than 10 percent leftover. This amount should go straight into a retirement fund. Many people have funds like these set up with their employers, but it is better to try and have your own in addition to, or in place of, so that you can ensure security with your money and that you are going to be getting the most back at the end of your career.

If you live like you don't have money, you'll have more later on. Though you might be able to afford the luxurious things in life, why do you have to indulge? Can't you find ways to cut costs and more humble methods of living that will ensure you have extra money to come to and use later on?

Remember the feeling of finding an old $10 or $20 bill in your winter coat pocket? Imagine being 80 years old and realizing you have over $200,000 left to use on whatever you want! Retirement can be a scary concept for many people as well. They think about being old, sick, or dying. It is only scary if you make it that way, so by ensuring that you have the money for this stage in your life, you'll end up being a lot less fearful of what's to come.

Sometimes, you might need to aim for more than 10 percent. If you live a luxurious lifestyle and plan to do the same in the future, you'll want to make sure that you are setting yourself up a little more than just the 10 percent.

The earlier you start saving, the less you will have to take away.

Some months don't have to be the same either if you are concerned at all about having to save too much. Try to give more than just 10 percent every paycheck, but if you can't, that's fine. Sometimes we have to put more money towards different costs, so we can't always fault ourselves for not being able to stay consistent.

Section off savings if you have more income to do so. If you are only using half your income to get by, put 25 percent towards retirement, 10 towards an emergency fund, and the remaining 15 towards a fund that you have specifically for investing. Now that you are aware of how much investment can help you now and, in the future, it is time to look more at the ways that you can start investing.

Chapter 2 – Invest in Yourself

Find the confidence needed to know that you only have to invest in yourself to make some real money. Not only do you have the intelligence to run your own company, but you can also be assured that you have a creative individuality to you that sets you apart from other people. There's something that we're all good at. Sometimes, it is easy to pinpoint, and other times, it takes more of an outsider's perspective or long reflection to figure out what it is that sets us apart from everyone else. Having the desire to take back of your finances and start investing is enough to make you realize your individuality. There are many people that will go on through their entire lives with no passion, desire, or motivation to do better. You know that not only do you want to do better, but you deserve to do better.

Look at your creative skills and see if there is something lucrative you can do with your own two hands. Are you good at drawing? Do you have a green thumb? Maybe music is your passion. Whatever it is that you can call your own, and is something that you enjoy doing, there's a way you can twist it to your benefit. If you can't sustain yourself from doing the craft alone, perhaps you could teach it. When we invest in ourselves, not only do we find ways to make money from something we enjoy doing, but we also grow ourselves from within by putting an emphasis on a personalized hobby. Instead of doing work for someone else all day long, you are working for yourself, so at the same time you are making money, you are becoming a better, healthier, and happier person.

Start treating yourself like an investment as well. Live healthier. Look at your life as an investment. You can eat unhealthily now, but it will be harder on your body the more you age. At the moment, you might not have any health problems, but there could be something in your life that you are doing that's reducing years from your expected life. Eating too many fatty foods can lead to heart disease. Smoking cigarettes is expensive and has a proven record of reducing life expectancy each time you light up a cigarette. These things are good, and we all have moments when we want to indulge the most. These habits also come back and affect you negatively as you get older. It is easier to think about the now and how we live our life because it is what's currently surrounding us. We can push the future out of our mind. We can't live like that anymore, so we have to see our bodies and minds as our own investments.

Find a positive outlook on this. You should be able to have the confidence necessary to know that you are the most powerful person in your life. What others say isn't always true, so don't get too hung up on trying to please others. There might be some people that won't or wouldn't invest in you, but that does not mean you don't still have value. If something isn't working, always try looking at it from a different perspective. There's always a way that you can turn something around in a positive way instead of abandoning it like a negative. You might sometimes feel as though you don't have much value, or that you've made a mistake, but you can put a positive twist on it that makes you feel better in the end.

Stop waiting around for something to happen. It is up to you to take charge of your financial life. Some people wake up in the morning thinking why they're so unhappy, and instead of doing anything about it, they keep going to the job they dislike and come home, too tired to do anything else except get ready for the next day. Other people realize they're unhappy and then look at what they can do to change, no matter how small. When you start investing in yourself and putting time into making yourself happier and healthier, you'll start to realize how much you've been missing out on.

Remember to never put too much pressure on yourself. You don't want to talk to yourself in a way that's demeaning or belittling. If we put too much pressure on ourselves, we end up being even harder when we don't live up to our high expectations. To make sure that we don't end up destroying our own self-esteem, we have to make sure that we're setting realistic goals, and accepting that sometimes, we're going to fail or miss deadlines. We know better than anyone else that we aren't perfect, but we also happen to be meaner to ourselves than we are to most other people. To make sure that we're not falling into a place of too much self-hate, we have to stick to things that are actually achievable. That is why it is so important to start with small savings and work your way towards putting more in the bank.

Studying and Focusing

Knowledge is power, especially when it comes to your own finances. The more you know about how to spend and save your money, the easier it will be for you to make informed decisions. Remember that not everyone can become an expert on finances overnight. You don't want to jump right into something you don't understand, because this is when mistakes can be made, and other mishaps will occur. Instead, make sure that you are knowledgeable about all aspects of a topic before jumping in. If you get in over your head, you'll only end up losing money, so it is important to be aware of everything necessary and become well-versed on how to handle any situation that could go wrong.

Remember that the more that you start to learn, the more you will realize you have so much more to learn. You can become very knowledgeable about real estate in a certain area, for example, but the more you immerse yourself in that area, the more you realize that you have a lot to learn about other places as well. It can be overwhelming to become more knowledgeable and aware about certain areas of investment because you'll feel as though you have so much left still to learn. What you should focus on instead is starting small and with the basics. Don't be afraid to look up the exact definition of certain words, even if you feel like you've heard them all your life. Make sure you understand things at their organic level, so you don't get too confused. The world of finance, especially with investments, can be filled with people that are more knowledgeable than you, and tricky as well, meaning you might end up getting caught in something that could have been avoided.

Choose your sources wisely. There's a lot of information out there that can be misleading, and there are others that will be too persuasive one way or another. When reading an article with "shocking" information, make sure you check all the sources, because more often than not, those headlines are just using hyperbole to get you to click and read more. Other sources will be in favor of a certain outcome, so they will paint the other side to be negative or scary, so you join their perspective. It is a tricky world on the internet to retain any information that's objective and correct. When it comes to your money, if you are not wary of how some media sources can twist things, you can end up losing money on your investments.

Focus only on your own goals, and no one else's. We all have different journeys and paths that we're going to go on and follow throughout our lives. What differs even more is the goal that's waiting at the end. Some of us know what we want in life from an early age, and the rest wander through, wondering what they want their goal to exactly be. Defining these parts of life can be challenging enough, so some people will latch onto the ideas and goals of others in an attempt to find relation on any level, desperate to find answers for the endless questions they have to confront. Don't get caught up on someone else's goals. Make sure that you are defining what you want and that you are taking the correct steps to get there, not to get to someone else's idea of what it means to be happy or successful.

Don't let too much fantasy get in the way. Especially don't let yourself follow any great fantasies. You have to stay realistic. It can be easy to get lost in the idea of what can be. Right now, you can fantasize about owning three cars, two houses, a boat, and a family that's picture perfect. All those ideas exist in our mind, and if we only think of all the good that comes along, we'll get lost in an idea, a fantasy. We have to make sure we're remaining grounded and not getting lost in the clouds of what could, maybe, potentially, possibly, be. Only stick to facts and take things in small steps so you can stay realistic. Your end goal is a general idea that will remain the same, but the smaller goals you make and follow on the way will alter a bit along your journey. For example, if one day you want to be a millionaire, that's something that you can't put an exact date on. You can, however, say, that you are going to have $25,000 in your savings by X date during X month in X year. That might alter by a month or two, but that's okay because you are still on track overall. This is realistic, but constant fantasy about what's going to happen when you become a millionaire can distract you from achieving the small goals necessary to get there.

If you need to find a business coach as well, don't be afraid to reach out to a professional. There are people who are trained in the business, their talent being that they can give an objective stance on what you need to do to find success. There are lawyers, bankers, accountants, and business managers that will help you when you need it. They are there to offer perspective and advice to make sure that you are spending your money in the smartest way possible. Some people would rather do things on their own, not fully trusting of someone else handling their money. Remember that this is their job and that though there are some bad people out there, you can trust trained professionals to do what's best. It is always advised to have someone there to help you at the beginning of your business and investment ventures, such as a business manager or a broker.

Building Belief and Passion

Sometimes, believing in ourselves can be the hardest part of overcoming our mistakes. While you might need someone to help you out in the beginning, that does not mean you aren't still capable of being your own boss down the road. When we go through life without accomplishing much, it can feel as though we aren't worth much, don't have success, or that we don't even deserve to do better. Even if you haven't found much success in your life yet, that does not mean that it is not still awaiting you if you stay determined and set achievable goals. It starts with believing that you are capable of anything, knowing that your past does not have to define what you do with your future.

We're taught that we have to depend on big businesses for money. We're robbed of our own beliefs. We see billionaires and other successful entrepreneurs, thinking that we don't have as great of an idea as them, or that we'll never be able to find that success. What's the point if we can't be the next Warren Buffet or Jeff Bezos? What we have to remember, however, is that everyone started small. No one is able to say that they were born successful, because having money does not define success. It is what you do with your resources, and how willing you are to face obstacles, that really matters when it comes to defining success.

We have to be humble with our goals. Some of us will get lucky at times, and we might get things that we would never have dreamt of at the beginning of the process. Throughout your investment journey, always think back to when you only had two dimes to rub together. There was a moment when you had less than what you do now, and if you aren't smart, you can get back to that point. Stay humble with who you are and never forget the journey before you found your success. When you can stay grounded and remember the reasons you started this in the first place, you'll find it is easier to stay true to yourself, which will lead to success down the road. Too many people find failure when they forget what the point of their mission was in the first place.

Who we surround ourselves with is important as well. Not everyone is going to be able to support you financially, but anyone that says they love or care about you is going to encourage and support you. Those that were there for you in the beginning are always going to be the most important. Someone that discourages you, devalues you, and invalidates you isn't going to be someone that helps you on your journey of investment. If you don't have people to support you, then it might end up being challenging to find and maintain success. Make sure you are surrounding yourself with people that matter the most and that you don't let anyone get in the way of accomplishing your dreams.

Passion is what's going to help drive you towards success. You have to care about the subject that you are investing in. When you do this, you can better ensure that you are actually caring about the outcome. You want to support what you are doing and stand behind the cause of what you are investing in. If you don't care about your investment, it is going to be harder to maintain relationships and keep up the earning momentum you are going through while establishing business with these varying investments. Those that don't have any desire to actively manage their investments won't be good leaders and can eventually become detached from their own business.

Having a lot of passion for our investments will also help ensure we have what it takes to keep going through when we might not have reached our ideal goals. If you easily give up because what you are participating in does not interest you, then you'll continually run into failure. Instead, we need to make sure that we're passionate about the subject of investment so that it is easier to keep up to date with the news and other innovations in the field. This is why investing in yourself can be so powerful. When you are doing something you care about, you'll find it much easier to be financially and emotionally invested into something.

Understanding the Game

You invest when you expect to get something in return, usually a lot more than the original investment. Making money from doing nothing other than giving money can sound like a great idea, but there's a lot more to it than just that. You have to make sure that you are looking at returns, work, time, and many other factors before agreeing to an investment. The game consists of finding the right balance between risk and safety, trust and deceit, and amount of effort. It is not as simple as just giving money and expecting to get some back in the end. It is how much you are going to get back; that is really worth it all in the end.

It is a tricky game that requires you to think smarter. You can't go into something without knowledge on the subject, or else you are going to find it very hard to actually make money. It is not something that's easy to discuss, but it is true that there are people out there that might take advantage of you. They know how to talk fast and positively about something to get you to buy into their idea. You can't always expect that this will help out in the end, however. Some people might take advantage of you and leave you with nothing even though they originally promised you everything.

Each type of investing has its own set of rules and regulations. There are laws in place that attempt to protect you from anything wrong. There are some people that still do things illegally and can sometimes encourage you to do the same. Remember that if something is illegal, it is never worth it in the end. You can't expect to find success if it involves cheating other people out of money or taking what is not yours. This goes beyond just legal, and into moral territory such as underpaid workers or employees that are asked to do too much for their specific task. You want to make sure that you are sticking to strong legal and moral standards so that you never have to worry about getting caught or hurting someone else. Investments are all about risk, but if the risk is getting caught doing something illegal, having to go to prison, or taking money that is not yours, it is never going to be worth the risk.

First and foremost, you want to make sure you are only doing legal investing. When working with other investors, make sure that you have your own separate legal team before working with them. You don't want to use only lawyers under their adviser because even lawyers can be swayed in one direction. Before making big investments, it is important you have someone legally on your side. This way, they can provide you with objective advice and important opinions that will protect you and your money.

There is a level of patience that you have to have as an investor. Though it is easy to just hope to throw all your money in at once and get a huge return, it is not how everything happens. You have to have patience and will power to take things slow at first to make sure you aren't making any mistakes. It can take years to save a certain amount of money, but it can all be lost if you throw it away in the wrong place. Don't let your hard work go down the drain by making a bad investment decision.

There's a balance between taking big risks and playing it safe as well. This is the hardest part of the game that you will have to get used to, and even the wealthiest and most successful investors won't find this balance to be easy to identify throughout their investments. Some things are just harder than others to judge, so you want to make sure that you are staying as objective as possible, while still having passion, and the guts, to take the right risk. Sometimes your risk will pay big, and other times, you might have to suffer a loss. This is all part of the game, however.

Common Investing Mistakes

Being unknowledgeable is the biggest mistake an investor can make. If you don't know enough about what you have decided to invest in, this is when people might start to take advantage of you. Other people, other experts, can sense when you might not know what you are doing, or even if you are trying to fake your knowledge on the subject to give the illusion you know more than what you do. Don't put yourself in a situation where someone can take advantage of your level of knowledge and experience.

If you are not completely aware of everything that goes into a company, you might end up making a big mistake. The more you can be aware of how a company operates before your investment, the more secure you can feel as you wait for the payout. If you rush into a decision before doing the right research and investigating, you'll end up losing out on a big investment.

Trying to prove a point, even if it is to yourself, might cause you to end up losing more money after all. It can be hard to admit that you were wrong about a gut-feeling, or that a business you hoped would pay big turned out to be a bust. You have to get used to sometimes admitting you are wrong so that you can pull your investments before you lose too much. If you keep waiting, hoping that you'll be right in the end, it can sometimes mean losing more than just your investment. Don't let your pride get the best of you.

Being too emotionally invested might alter your perception. It is always best to be as objective as possible. If it is your own business, this can sometimes hurt you if you are not objective enough. Even harder can sometimes be investing in a friend's or family's business. When you want something to work so bad, you can sometimes become blind to the obvious red flags that are warning you not to invest.

Not planning is a mistake many people make. Being too rigid with goal-meeting might hurt you, but you want to make sure that you have an idea of how you are going to achieve your objectives.

Sticking to other people's advice can also mean that you might not be making the best decisions for yourself. It is good to hear from the experts and to learn from your own mistakes, but you also need to make sure that you are focusing on yourself and doing what's best for you and your money.

Chapter 3 – The Right Mindset

Look at the mindset you've had before you started investing to determine where things could have potentially gone wrong. Did you create goals too high? Did you make unrealistic predictions? Were you unknowledgeable about the subject that you tried investing in? Remember that all of these things are under the common mistakes that we just discussed. You have to use these guidelines as your basis for preparing your investment plans. If you aren't careful with how you find the right investing mindset, you'll end up setting yourself back, making it harder to achieve your goals in the end.

Make sure you are in the right place physically to have the right mentality needed for success. Sometimes, this means moving to a different location, maybe where your business is more needed or accepted. Perhaps there is nothing around you that's going to be worth investing in. It starts with looking at your surroundings to make sure that what's going on inside will be achievable.

Have the confidence to take in both the good and the bad. There are going to be moments when you might have been wrong, so will you be willing to admit your mistakes? There is going to be a time when you lose money with your investment, and it won't feel great. However, when you do make money, it's going to feel awesome, so you have to be ready and prepared to find that balance, and handle both the good and the bad that can come along with investing.

Be ready for criticism for your investments as well. If it's your own business especially, it might be hard not to take it personally when someone criticizes your business. You have to stay objective, however, and take in this criticism so that you can actually improve your business for the better.

Don't push yourself too far into goals that aren't achievable. Remember that this isn't going to be healthy for an investing mindset. It's easy to fantasize about what's at the finish line, but don't forget to also focus on the path that it takes to get there. Are you in the right mindset to differentiate between what you want and what is actually possible to be achievable? If you can't figure out if your goals are realistic or not, ask yourself if they're things that you would assign to a family member, friend, or someone else you love. If it seems ridiculous for someone else to achieve, why would you put so much pressure on yourself to achieve that certain goal? Don't push yourself harder than you would someone else because this is how you're setting yourself up for failure.

Remember that waiting around only elongates the process. The best time to start is right now. Sometimes, we get scared to start, because we're not ready to handle what might happen if things don't turn out our way. Part of an investing mindset involves making sure you're emotionally prepared and stable enough to take everything in, no matter if it's going to be good or bad.

Overcome the Fear of the Unknown

Fear is what is going to hold you back the most. If you're too fearful about what might happen, you're not going to have what it takes to make sure that you go through with your plans. Don't spend too much time on what might happen and make sure that instead, you're imagining the benefits that can come along as well.

We spend more time on the "what ifs," rather than what is actually happening. You might find that you have anxious thoughts and fears of what could go wrong that span over a longer period of time than what the actual investment endures. Don't let yourself get caught up on something that scares you and remember that there's a chance of good happening every time you picture what could go wrong.

Part of overcoming fear is understanding why it is there in the first place. Fear isn't always a bad thing. It can be what drives our passion in the first place. Fear over our future, fear over taking care of our family, and fear over not having our own basic human needs met can cause us to expand a part of our brain that thinks creatively and logically to come up with a solution to our problems. If we didn't ever have fear, we might not have as much motivation, and not enough would get done. Too much fear, however, can be just as blinding as it is encouraging, so we can't let it take over our minds too much in the investing process.

Making yourself more knowledgeable will help ensure you are less fearful. When you are aware enough about a certain topic to have the confidence to carry it out, then you will make sure that you don't have to continually second guess yourself or wonder if you're making the wrong decision. If you're misinformed, you're going to misjudge, which can result in a mishap. Instead, be smart in all aspects to find success in the end.

Starting small and practicing is a great way to build confidence as well. There are different investing apps that present information in fun games, so try out something new if you think that you're not feeling confident with your level of knowledge. There are stock apps that can help get you well versed on the idea of that area of investing as well. Watch TV shows about real estate if that is your area of investment. Practicing and becoming aware is going to be a good first step on the path towards investment.

Find ways to look at mistakes and accidents in a practical sense. Plan out mistakes before they even happen so you can come up with solutions should you run into that issue. By doing this, you're making yourself aware of what not to do while also alleviating fear by coming up with a new plan. The more prepared you are, the easier it will be to make the most informed decision possible for your money.

When we start accepting "the worst", it becomes a lot less scary if it might actually happen. Think of what is the worst that could happen. With an investment of $10,000, the worst that could happen is that you lose that money. Don't go beyond that. Don't factor in interest or anything else lost, because it's over now and there's nothing you can do but use this experience as a learning one.

Stepping Out of the Comfort Zone

Sometimes the scariest part of investing is when we have to step outside our spending comfort zone. We're used to a certain method of spending as it is, but when it comes to saving money for investing, things have to change. If we take away something we're used to, such as a music service subscription or even getting a Starbucks coffee every morning, we can start to get worried about what will happen now that things are different. Don't let your fear of change hold you back from making the right choices.

Breaking habits is another scary thing for many people. When we go off track from what we're used to, our natural instinct is to get worried, because this might disrupt everything else in our life. Make sure that you remind yourself that change is going to be what helps carry you to success, and it won't always be your downfall.

Don't be tempted by anything that seems too safe, or as if there are no risks. When something gets set up this way, it's usually not worth the payoff, or not legitimate altogether. All investments have risks, no matter how small. If someone tries to cover that up, it might not be legit, so don't let your desire for comfort and stability lead to an inability to make the right and best-informed decision.

Familiarize yourself with what makes you scared to change. Is it something in your childhood that has caused you not to want to pursue anything different, or are you just worried that you're going to end up without any money? When we confront why it is that we might not be interested in change, it will make it easier to overcome these fears so we can actually achieve all that we have been working towards.

Self-reflection will be an important part of this process. You have to look back and ask yourself if you took a big enough risk. Are you playing it safe because you're being cautious, or are you just too scared to make what you believe is the best decision? You have to start asking yourself the hard questions so you can start to really see your life turn around in a different direction.

Change happens from risk, whether it is big or small. If everything stayed the same way it always has been, we'd all still be living on the land without electricity. That might be the way some people want to do things, but others depend on cars, electronics, and everything else involved in our present and future. We have to be willing and ready to accept change, and this only occurs when we step outside our comfort zone.

Let change be your new comfort. Start to fear the old, because it can mean that nothing ever gets better! What's comfortable isn't always what's best for you, as it's just what you're used to. Don't let yourself settle for this anymore. You deserve so much more, and the way that you're going to get it is by stepping outside your box. Look at what defines you and expand on that to allow for new ideas and innovations to flood your past and prepare for a bigger and brighter future.

Understanding Your Personal Level of Risk

What we are willing to risk will differ from person to person. You might have a family to care for, people that depend on you, and some assets that you just can't go without. You could also be someone that doesn't have much to lose at all. These are two different situations, so you can't expect that both will warrant the same amount of risk.

How much risk we can get away with will also differ among various individuals. Make a list of all the things that you have to lose in order to determine what your level of risk might be. This is both financially as well as in your life overall. Your list might include your $2,000 savings, your relationship with your spouse or family, or your morals in general. The longer your list of risk, the more you have to be considerate of everything bad that could come along with a certain investment.

Before making an investment, you have to make a risk assessment. What's the most that you could possibly lose? If it's not worth it to you, if you lose more than half of what you have, or if you just don't want to lose anything at all, then don't go ahead with the investment. If you make a decision without a risk assessment, you're going to find that you end up making poor decisions more often.

Take small risks at first. Don't put all your eggs in one basket, and don't expect to find huge success overnight. As you start with smaller risks, you'll also be able to better assess your ability to handle loss, and what it means when something doesn't turn out as you might have planned. By doing this, we can become more accustomed to loss, so it doesn't hit so hard if we do have to experience this feeling.

Don't do anything based on emotion. You have to be smart with your risks. It's good to be passionate about your investments and to care about how something might turn out either way, but if you're too emotionally invested, you might end up making ill-informed decisions. Make sure that you haven't put too much emotional risk on something. If you're acting hastily, then it won't be the best objective decision for you at the current moment.

Don't look at investing as a form of gambling. "You win some, you lose some," isn't always the right mentality for larger risks. You will win some, and you will lose some, but it's not as simple as that. Look at why you won and why you lost to figure out what you need to do better, or the same, the next time around. When we assess our risk, we can make sure that we're winning much more often than we end up losing.

Long-Term Mentality

You have to find the right shift in your money mentality, and you have to accept that there's no going back. Once you realize how important it is to save, then it can be much easier to actually start to do this. Look at your life and ponder on what it was that made it so important that you started to read this book in the first place. Now use that as your core value for continuation. Remind yourself that there's no going back and that you're not just doing this to make you feel better now, but that you're doing this because there is no other option. You can't go back to the way things used to be anymore. From here on out, you have to start saving. This kind of long-term mentality is what's going to be the most crucial for keeping up with success. It can be easy to start sometimes, but it can be even harder to keep up with those changes once you shifted the way you think, act, and spend your money.

You can't just plan for the now. Investing is all about planning for the future. If you have kids, this should be even more inspiration for you to start investing. If you have a health issue that you know will make things worse in the long run, this is another reason why you should be passionate about saving. Even just having someone you love next to your side should be enough, as we should strive to provide the best life possible for those that we plead our devotion to. If you don't have a reason to invest, then it will be harder to keep up with what you need to do in order to make sure that you're consistently putting away money. It isn't always another person that's going to be your reason for investing. This is common, but you should be investing in yourself as well. You deserve to have financial security after living a long and happy life. Don't give up on yourself.

Remember that you are responsible for what's going to happen. There are going to be moments when you get lucky, and sometimes, you might end up having some money fall into your lap. However, we can't just wait for these moments. We can't live life from one hope to the next. At some point, we have to take the wheel and direct our life. That doesn't mean we'll never find luck again. Random chances and added bonuses are still going to be there if we don't wait around for them. In the meantime, take charge and change your life, and your finances, for the better. Only we know what's best for us, so we can't just hope and wish that someone else does the work for us.

Always look for the best outcome, not just the one that's going to get you by. It's easy to be average, that's why it's referred to as 'average.' That's not what's going to be the most fulfilling in your life, however. You need to make sure that you're striving for more than just what you need to get by. Surviving is important, but what's the point if you're not aiming even higher? You can live for years, but if you're not fulfilled, not fully enjoying those experiences, are you really even living in the end?

Remember to be committed to the hustle. If it were easy, everyone would be an investor with a ton of money. That's not how the world works, however, so set yourself apart by making the strive for more money your main passion. When you set your mind to something, you can stay dedicated to it only if you believe in that goal, believe in yourself, and have passion about the journey. If you lose sight of your true self, or why you started on this journey in the first place, you're only making it harder for you to achieve your dreams.

Put an emphasis on the outcome and not just the challenge. It can be easy to pick out the challenging parts of the investment journey. You might have to give up something you like, and you could lose out on some money. That's enough to scare a lot of people away. Don't let yourself forget, however, that you could end up getting everything you ever wanted if you're just willing to try.

Think Simple

Sometimes, when it comes to investing, we overthink things and end up deeper than when we started. It's important to be knowledgeable about everything that you're going to invest in, but if you get too hung up on some of the logistics, you can end up setting yourself back a bit further. Don't get caught up on the "what ifs" and instead make sure you're looking logically and objectively at everything that you might be dedicating your time to.

Start small with where you are going to save. Remember that all it takes is putting a few dollars into a savings account every week. The more you make, the more you can put away, and the more you put away, the more the interest that will be gained on your overall investment. No matter how challenging it might be to do the smallest thing, remember that it will always get easier over time. Don't give up on yourself or your abilities to find success.

When coming up with new investment ideas, think simply. Take an idea that already exists and find a way to put a twist on it. Sometimes you don't always have to think completely organically to find the right idea for an investment that works for you. Instead of throwing away old ideas that don't work, look for a way that you can take that idea and spin it positively. More often than not, you'll find that a fresh perspective is all it takes to think of something amazing.

Just say "no." It is about as simple as you can get with words. When you want to spend money on something and you're not sure if it's the right decision, just say no. When your gut is telling you that an investment doesn't sound right, just say no. If you find that you're only saying no, then you might need a change. For the most part, however, this simple word can protect us from the wrong decision. There will be other chances, so don't be afraid to use that word.

If something does not feel right, it is probably not. It is as simple as that. Our gut has those feelings because it's sensing something that our brain has yet to pick up on. Most of the time, you'll save yourself from a mistake and be happy that you didn't put yourself in a position that was challenging to come out of.

Look at a dollar as the dollar. Never tell yourself, "It's only this much amount of money." A dollar is a dollar, and that's enough money. You need to take risks, but if you're making a decision with the sense that money is disposable, you aren't making the most informed decision. A loss is a loss no matter how big or how small.

Enjoy the Process

Nothing is ever worth anything if you are completely miserable in the process. If you hate cars but just invested in a used-auto dealership, you're going to have a terrible time! When you're unhappy, it's a lot harder to make the right informed decisions for your business or investment.

Passion is going to be your most powerful tool. When you actually care about something, you won't be distracted by other fantasies of a better life. Think of how hard it can be to work or study sometimes because you're so busy wishing you were somewhere else. When you're exactly where you want to be, you won't have to fantasize so much.

Learn to enjoy the thrill that comes along and drop the anxiety that holds you back. You might go through some scary moments of anxiety when waiting to see if an investment will pay off or not, but don't always look at that as a bad thing. Sometimes, that adrenaline that results from an investment is good for us and helps us realize what's important.

If something isn't right for you, move on. Don't try to convince yourself that you're happy or trick yourself into believing you're passionate about something you're not. Life is far too short to pretend we're happy.

When you are unhappy, too much emotion gets involved. The best way to make sure you're putting money towards the right investments and also that you're operating business properly is to make sure that you're actually happy during this process.

Life is easier all around when we learn to enjoy the process of everything, not just how we handle our finances. Look for the good in the bad, because it will be there. One cannot exist without the other, so even the most negative experiences hold a bit of light.

Chapter 4 – Start Soon, but Start Small

The longer we wait to get started, the more return we're going to need to set us up for the future. This isn't just in the amount that we end up putting away, but the potential interest that our savings and investments could make as well. If you have money put away at this moment into your savings, it can make a lot more money between now and ten years, when we might have normally started saving. It is never too soon to put money away. Even if you don't want to wait until you are 65 or higher to touch your retirement fund, you'll still have more money if you need to go on vacation in your 40s or buy a new house before you retire. We should aim to save this for retirement, but if not, it is always better to have money put away rather than to spend it on meaningless things now.

The mentality of pushing things off is what gets so many people in trouble. Before you realize it, you'll be getting close towards retirement, potentially wondering where you are going to get your money from. It is not even about retirement either. You might be mid-thirties wondering how you are going to send your kids to school or questioning if you are going to die before you are able to pay off your student loans. It is never fun to have to be responsible! It is always more exciting to buy the new bag or keep upgrading your car. It is not the smart thing to do, however. You have to start treating your future self better than how you are taking care of yourself right now so that you don't have to worry in the future about what you are going to do when it comes to your finances.

If we start off right away by doing too much, we'll end up putting ourselves in a place of disappointment. If you put all your $5,000 savings towards one investment next week, and that investment goes nowhere and you lose all your money, you are going to be disappointed and discouraged, wanting to give up and never invest again. Instead, start small, with an investment less than 10 percent of your savings. If you keep things small and simple, you'll "win" more and find consistent success that will give you the power and encouragement needed for the right mindset. If you keep risking and losing, you'll never have the desire to keep going.

The bigger the risk, the bigger the return, but also the potential for a bigger loss. You have to take risks when it comes to investing. You won't always be able to make as big of risks as you want, and sometimes you are going to question if you should have put more towards certain investments. It takes practice to get to the right level of risk/return/loss. This is why you should start small. Imagine it like being a runner. You would start in smaller races first before you go for the biggest one of your area, right? Because you know that it takes practice to be the best and that if you go too big, you'll fail even bigger and it might be too hard to pick yourself back up and start over.

It is good to be eager in the beginning, but we also have to make sure that we're being smart. Excitement, passion, and a high sense of hope are necessary to actually see a return in your investments, but all those things can also be blinding, so we have to make sure we find the right balance.

There are two rules to this game: compound interest and not losing money.

Compound Interest

Compound interest is essentially interest on the interest that already exists. There's an amount that your investment will earn, and there is also an amount of interest that will be earned on that amount. If you leave your investments alone for a longer time, most commonly your savings, then this is how they will have the potential to grow faster, longer.

Your money earns interest. If you put your money in a savings account, it earns a certain amount of money just for sitting there, especially due to inflation. If you have a retirement fund, this will also gain an interest amount. Compound interest, then, is the interest that is earned on that amount. This is always something that will be important for investors to remember to calculate.

It also earns a higher rate because it just sits there, so as a dollar grows, so does the value of the principal.

Example

In order to determine if you are making the right investment, you have to ensure that you are earning the right amount of compound interest to fulfill your goals. The formula for determining this is:

$A = P (1 + r/n)\ \hat{}(nt)$

A is your compound interest.

P is the principal amount.

r is the interest rate, and for this, you would use a decimal.

N is the number of times that interest will be compounded each year.

nt is the time in years of the investment.

Let's look at an example of this. Let's say that you invest $7,000 for ten years with an interest rate of 5% a year.

The formula would then be A = 7000 $(1+.05 / 12)$ ^$(12(10))$

Compound interest would then be 11,529.07.

Don't Lose Money

With investments, we have to make sure that we're actually gaining money and not just keeping a consistent, steady flow of money. If interest and inflation even each other out, then there won't be any point for investing.

Along with compound interest, you have to make sure that the money is worth something more than the original investment in the end. Sometimes, we don't realize that our money isn't actually making money at all, and that instead, the income is consistent.

Examples

In order to make sure that your money is actually going to be making more money with your investment, there is a formula you can use to make sure that you are not going to be losing money.

You'll want to make sure that after a long period of time, you are going to have actually gained money. To make sure that a long-term investment is worth it, use this formula to see how long it will take to double your investment. This is known as the rule of 72.

The formula is 72/the interest rate.

It seems simple, and it is. If you have an investment of $10,000, and there's a 6 percent interest rate, you would take 72/6. That equals 12, so it will take 12 years for your $10,000 to turn into

$20,000.

You have to ask yourself when investing if this makes your investment worth it. You would be making a little over $1,000 each year, but if you are working every week on that investment, it is likely not worth it.

Chapter 5 – Diversification

In this chapter, we're going to give you quick hints on diversification, but you should strive to read more advanced books on the subject once you start investing in an area that you enjoy.

This is the path that many investors follow to make sure they have a diverse selection of investments. If you find more than one investment to make, then that's going to be a better way to spend your money rather than putting all that money towards just one investment.

You won't be able to diversify in the beginning. You might not have enough money to make more than one investment, so you'll have to start small. Eventually, it should be your goal to try and make as many investments as possible.

It should be your goal to expand to other markets. If you've only invested in stocks, it might be time to take your money elsewhere so you can really grow. Perhaps you've always been interested in the restaurant industry, or perhaps you want to invest in a retail store. Diversification comes later on when we have extra money to have the security to make investments we might not have made in the beginning.

This also means investing in areas other than the one that you might be the most knowledgeable about. You'll still want to be as knowledgeable as you would with everything else, but it's still good to expand on your areas of comfort so that you're getting the widest spread possible for your money.

Different kinds of investments are important in making a diverse selection of business. If you only put investments into different restaurants, then you might find a consistent fluctuation of money coming in. Try a different kind of investment, such as one that involves investing in one person, or a smaller business. You'll find you make money in a different way than if you would have stuck to the same kind of business.

Diversification as Risk Management

The reason this is important is so that you don't put all your eggs in one basket. This is a common quote that references the disaster that would happen if you were to drop that one basket. All your eggs would break if they were in the same basket. However, if you have 10 eggs in three different baskets, then you'll still have 6 or 7 good ones should you drop just one basket. It's possible you might still drop all three baskets, but your chances will be much lower than if you just drop the one.

Diversification ensures that you don't risk losing all your money if one thing falls through. By using this form of risk management, you are ensuring that you won't have to worry as much when deciding whether or not to take a big risk. You can take a chance on one investment because your five other investments are still secure.

Diversification won't matter if all your investments are in the same industry. If you put all your money towards different swimsuit stores, then if the weather is bad all summer, you didn't make any money. However, if you invested in a swimsuit store, a coat store, a shoe store, and even a restaurant, the bad summer won't hurt your finances as much.

This is also why it is so important to make sure you are knowledgeable about many different topics and not just one. Sometimes, diversification can actually set you back, so you have to be careful with spreading yourself too thin. Don't try to do too much, and add diversification slowly as you grow your businesses.

Potential Areas to Invest

Once you've saved your money, it is time to decide where to invest those savings. You probably want to start with what you're most knowledgeable about. If you've worked in a hair salon all your life, this could be an area you choose to invest. As you grow your money, you can start spreading that cash to other areas.

Start by looking at how you can invest in yourself. You know yourself better than anyone, and you have the skills it takes to complete a task without having to hire outside help.

Make sure you choose something that you are knowledgeable and passionate about. Look at your goals and set realistic ideas of what you want from your investments. If you want to become a millionaire, investing in a small business might not seem like a big idea, but it could be a good place to start.

Make sure that there will be room for diversification. Don't choose something in such a niche that you'll never be able to diversify in other areas.. For example, if you decide to only give money to a leather sex toy shop, some family businesses might not want to work with you later on. Don't let this fear hold you back, as you should do what you're passionate about. However, be realistic with how current businesses might affect future businesses as well.

It is best to make sure that you can also find ways to invest in the long-term. If it's just a startup company, this might not be your first investment. You might want to start with something that's already a little more established to make sure that you can find long-term goals. Once you have security from those smaller and more stable investments, diversification can start, and you can expand to areas you didn't thought of in the beginning.

Stock

Stock is a popular form of investment because you are putting money towards more money. It's a complicated industry, so make sure you study more materials on this subject before diving right in.

This is also a very competitive market and one that you have to be sure you are prepared for. Investing in companies you like is also important, but you don't want to be too focused on something you like if it does not offer the best benefits.

Make sure to calculate the risk that you are able to take before purchasing certain stocks. Sometimes, you end up losing more money than just what you invested if you're not careful.

Use money specifically for stocks, and don't treat it like a gamble. Though it can be like a slot machine sometimes with certain chances, you can't look at stocks the same way you would something with random risk.

Use practice methods before you start investing, such as a stock app that mimics the actual market.

Real Estate

Real estate is a great form of investment as well because people will always need a place to live. You can start simply by buying empty lots and holding onto them until they cost more, selling when the price is higher due to the surrounding up-and-coming businesses.

Flipping houses is becoming a more and more popular form of investment and can be a fun and creative way to expand your finances.

Find ways that you can rent your own home. Apps like Air Bnb help you become an entrepreneur. Always be smart with where you decide to put your real estate money, and make sure to do plenty of research before going down this avenue of investment.

Conclusion

"It takes 20 years to build a reputation and five minutes to ruin it. If you think about that, you'll do things differently." – Warren Buffet

You have the ability to take control of your finances, no matter how differently you might feel. Even if you don't understand money, interest, investing, or stocks, you are still going to be able to take charge over your life and gain control of your own money rather than depending on someone else to make a dime. No one was born knowledgeable about how to spend money. Some people are born rich, and others are born poor, and while that can seriously determine whether or not you'll have money in your life, it isn't always indicative of how well you'll understand money in your life.

If you save money, you can build your way as an investor. It only takes a few dollars a week to start a savings account, and once you have an amount to invest, you can end up getting double or more your original investment. There's a lot to do in between initial investment and assessing returns, but you have to remember that it still all starts with saving money in the first place.

It all starts by consolidating and cutting out unnecessary spending. Everyone has at least one expense they can cut out of their life. Some people might find that they save hundreds of dollars a week if they get smart with their money, and other people will find that they're already doing their best to cut down on unnecessary fluff. No matter what situation you might be in, remember that there is always room to save more money.

Saving ten percent of your income is a great way to make sure you are preparing for retiring. You might have to save more than ten percent based on your current income and how you expect to live after retirement, but you also want to ensure that you are doing your very best to save $10 for every $100 that you are making so that you have money to spend on your future, in the future.

Investing in yourself can seem scary, but it is a great method to make extra money. When you work with just yourself and invest in only you, that's when you can have complete control over your finances and ensure that you are in charge of making money.

Studying and focusing will be your keys to making sure that you are finding success in your field. Never stop reading new books about investing, and always keep updated with the latest news when it comes to global and more geographically specific economics.

Building belief and passion are important to make sure that you are going to be making the wisest decisions with your money. If you don't believe in yourself and lack passion in the thing that you've invested money in, you'll never find true happiness or success with your money endeavors.

Understanding the game can be a challenge, but it is what you need to do to make sure that you are spending your money the right way. There are plenty of legal rules put in place to protect your money and the money of others. There are also just as many unspoken rules about the game that sometimes, you might end up learning things the hard way. The more prepared you are going into an investment, the higher is the chance that you will come out on top in the end.

It is important to make sure that you are aware of common investing mistakes so that you don't make them yourself. There will be some times when you have regrets or moments you wish you had done things differently. Always remember, however, that it is better to learn from other people's mistakes so that you don't have to make them all on your own.

The right mindset is what's going to be important in ensuring that you are making the proper investments. All the money in the world won't be able to save you from yourself if you don't believe in your abilities and the things that you are investing in.

Fear is going to be your biggest obstacle. It is what's going to hold you back from making the right decision, and it might be what pushes you over the edge towards making a decision that isn't good for you or your money.

Stepping out of your comfort zone won't be easy, but it is the only way to make sure that you are actually eliciting change. We can't keep doing the same things we've always done and expect to get any results that might be different.

Your personal level of risk is different from anyone else's risk. While it is good to look at other people's methods of investing to determine what not to do, you also have to remember that your level of risk is going to be different from everyone else's.

The long-term mentality is important to find in order to make sure that you are not messing up down the road. The point of investing is looking towards the future, so we have to make sure that we're setting ourselves up for success later on and not just putting an emphasis on what's best in the 'now'.

Think simply rather than in too much of a complex manner. Some things will require you to work and think harder, but you are also going to have moments where it is most important that you look at something in a simple, logical sense. Trust your gut and listen to your head. Anything else might complicate the process and cause you to make the wrong decision just because you were overthinking things.

Enjoy the process, or else you are going to make yourself unhappy down the road. If you work too hard and focus too much on your investments and the money that you are making, it is only going to cause stress, and you might not find the happiness that you were searching for in the first place. Remember, there's a reason why you've chosen to invest, so don't let anything else stop you from achieving your dreams.

Start soon, but make sure that you also start small. It is your money, so you are not necessarily going to want to jump into the deep end right away. Instead, wade a bit before diving so that you can be sure you won't get yourself into any situations that are harder to come out of.

Compound interest is essential to ensure that you don't lose any money. These are going to be the two most important things that you'll have to look out for as you invest in your future.

Diversification is a form of risk management. The more you can spread out your money, the bigger security net would be in place to catch you when you fall. Look at all your options when determining where to invest. Real estate is a great form of investment that seems to be becoming more and more popular.

For more information on this topic, look out for my next book that will fill you in even more and help to take your investments to the next level.

www.ingramcontent.com/pod-product-compliance
Lightning Source LLC
Chambersburg PA
CBHW020711180526
45163CB00008B/3037